COOLEY THE ANT "A HIP HOP STORY"

Written by: Jeffrey E. Jones (Jazz Matazz) & James K. Allen (Spoatymac)

Illustrated by: James K. Allen (Spoatymac)

Edited by: Theresa J. Gonsalves

Text Copyright © 2016 by: Jeffrey E. Jones
Illustrations Copyright © 2016 by: James K. Allen

ISBN: 978-0-692-63419-6

Library of Congress Control Number: 2016902665

No part of the publication may be reproduced in whole or in part or stored in a retrieval system or transmitted in any form or by any means eletronical, mechanical, photocopying, recording or otherwise, without permission of the publisher.

Published by: F.C.E. PUBLISHING

All Rights Reserved.

Spoatymac is a Talladega College alumnus, author, illustrator and music producer with a collection of Hip Hop LP's on-line...
@ http://www.cdbaby.com/cd/spoatymac and
@ http://www.amazon.com/Spoatymac/e/B001LIEUE2.

For book signings or to place an order, please email your request to heatcity702@gmail.com

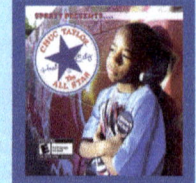

Jazz Matazz is a Grambling State University alumnus poet, author and publisher who has been featured in various urban publications. He has also written and published three books of poetry. His work can be found on www.amazon.com

Spoatymac – I would like to thank my Moma Verna Allen & Uncle Greg Coleman for motivating me to continue drawing and recording music, Jazz Matazz for assisting with bringing Cooley's story to life and everyone around the world who has followed me on my journey to success. This book is dedicated to my lovely wife Alonda, my beautiful daughter Asia and my loving family.

Jazz Matazz – I would like to thank Spoatymac for including me in his vision, Theresa J. Gonsalves for her knowledge and expertise, as well as my wife Kim and daughter Ky Ky for their continued support.

SPECIAL THANKS TO OUR FAMILY, FRIENDS AND FANS THAT SUPPORTED US THROUGHOUT OUR VARIOUS ACCOMPLISHMENTS!

F.C.E. PUBLISHING

A couple raps of delight to entice his friends.
They were so surprised, they both joined in.

Cooley's parents had a chat with him. They were worried! He rapped all day but not a crumb had been buried.

Then they told him, "the winter is sure to be long. If he gathered no food and just wrote rap songs."

Cooley's friends had to quit too because the music wasn't helping to collect much food.

They took a trip to the window and they couldn't believe, Cooley chased his dreams and WOW he's on TV!

COOLEY THE ANT

But wait! There's more... →

PARENTS, help your child unscramble the words by using the word box below.

COOLEY THE ANT
The Hip Hop Story

1. YOLCEO _____
2. FO LYS _____
3. IPMSANT _____
4. POH IPH _____
5. RWETIN FEEZER _____
6. ADERM GBI _____
7. YCNLOO KELYEW _____

8. DUAGYLB _____
9. BLEMBU EBE _____
10. EATM KRWO _____
11. HDRA OWRK _____
12. IARLPLATAC _____
13. AETRH MROW _____
14. OADRI WHSO _____

WORD BOX

LADY BUG	COLONY WEEKLY	CATAPILLAR
WINTER FREEZE	COOLEY	RADIO SHOW
PMANTIS	DREAM BIG	SO FLY
TEAM WORK	BUMBLE BEE	HIP HOP
HARD WORK		EARTHWORM

COOLEY'S WORDSEARCH

PARENTS, help your child, find and circle each of the words from the list below.
Words may appear fowards, backwards, horizontally, vertically or diagonally in the grid.

```
S M A E R D R U O Y G N I S A H C O P L
M G P U N Q O G F T I X F C J W F P O R
D J E D O X Z M D J M U T S I T N A M P
T Z Y P A A R O R L P F M T M R O O A X
O S D R A W A C I S U M T C E S N I Y C
D A H E A E O O E E U W J X P T E Y R O
C E K R O W D R A H C Z X Y T U Z H O L
E M N K J U M D V A J P Y M I T E K T O
D H L I F I F N D M B I F O I S E U S N
N A M D O O F G N I R E H T A G R E P Y
X X Q D F I O C Y F T U P E D C F I O W
D F E T N A E H T Y E L O O C D R B H E
N S E M F Y R K R O W M A E T F E O P E
I E E N S U D T S S D O O E E V T A I K
Y L F O S P B N Y O E J C N I X N B H L
X D O O Q M A Q N Y R N A N N Z I E M Y
T H I H M A K I N G M U S I C M W F P U
T G M Z U G Y N X N E Z T P T O N O M C
```

COOLEY THE ANT   WINTER FREEZE   COLONY WEEKLY   P MANTIS   HIP HOP STORY
GATHERING FOOD   HARD WORK   CHASING YOUR DREAMS   INSECT MUSIC AWARDS
TEAM WORK   MAKING MUSIC   SO FLY

www.ingramcontent.com/pod-product-compliance
Lightning Source LLC
Chambersburg PA
CBHW061818290426
44110CB00026B/2907